Goodbyes We Don't Expect

Faraway

If you're reading this,
you are still breathing:
there is a reason for that.

Chapters:

Summer Rain

Right now, I feel awful.
But If I can make it through these first hours,
these first days and weeks and months…if I can
just live, survive, be alive, through these endless
rows and columns of sad moments, I'll know that I
can outlast anything. I'll know that I can be the one
standing in the end - not these thoughts in my head
that tell me to give up before my next breath.

And I plan to hold on. I'm betting everything on
the hope that I'll always have the strength to get
out of whatever state I'm in, that I'll always be
stronger than the way I feel at times - victorious
over any "right now" that towers over me.

- how to survive a moment

In those last days,
I'm not mad that you
still said "*I love you*."
What bothers me is
how you said it so
convincingly.

We'd fight into the
depths of early morning,
pointing fingers and showing
each other our wounds. Because,
it's so difficult to admit that you're
the one who is wrong, and it's just
so damn easy to hand over blame
to anyone other than yourself.

I thought we could change the world together,
but all you ever did was tell me how badly I needed
to change myself. And what started as something so
beautiful slowly became the source of my insecurities.
In the end, I was such a fool for you, I almost let you
make me believe forever that who I was wasn't
something to be proud of.

- in love and blindfolded

I wanted you to be the purpose
for all of the pain in my past so badly,
I let you hurt me in ways very similar
to the ways of people before you.
All it took was me telling myself,
"this is different; this is not
somewhere I've been before."

- to keep my head in the clouds

I tried to love you
through it all, and you
shut off as if you were born
with a self-destruct button
somewhere near your heart
for moments like these.

- when the lights went out

I didn't just lose
my soulmate; I lost
my best friend, too.

I'll probably spend
the rest of my life just
trying not to call you.

People always said
we'd never last forever,
and, sadly, in the end,
we proved them right.

- I bet they laugh at us

You left as if it
were just another
Monday afternoon.

It's just crazy to me
how we'd rather flush
years down the drain
instead of try harder to
love and understand
each other.

I've been running away
from anything we did together –
staying up all night just to avoid
the very sun that touched us when
we first touched each other. I feel its
warmth against my skin, and that
still hits a little too close to home.

- all alone in my hideaway

Trusting in someone is like
standing on glass and hoping
it doesn't cave in and break.

And through this glass, you can
see the chaos, what could happen
someday, unfolding below you.

But you stand there, your feet
planted firmly on the glass, your
views on this person still intact.

And you wait there, suspended
inches above the end, awaiting the
day wherein your trust is so deep,
the glass is so thick, you no longer
see the chaos lurking below you.

  - trust: the heart's leap of faith

It's just a little ironic that
the person who's the cause
of all this pain I feel was once
my answer to the question,
"will I ever be happy again?"

Life is so weird without you. I have all of this love
but no one to give it to anymore. I have all of this time
in my days with no one to fill them up with. I can't seem
to remember much lately, as if my soul is too distracted to
be here in the moment - as if it's still where you are. And
I'm just not sure whether I should be happy that I loved
something so much that it washed over me like a tidal wave
when it was over, or if I should be planning my escape
from this loneliness to be back in your arms again.

- today feels like a room with nothing in it

And now I'm left here, wondering
what hurts more: the fact that I was
not who you dreamt up in your head,
or the fact that you were so selfish in
who you hoped I'd be, you didn't even
attempt to accept who I truly was.

- when it was all said and done

I always felt like
the backbone of our
conversations: if I fell,
everything fell with it.

- *thinking of things to talk about*

I'll never understand
how we fit so much love
inside of such a short
amount of time.

I miss falling asleep
knowing I belonged
somewhere.

- somewhere was with you

You don't want to be in my life anymore,
and I'm still so confused as to why that is.
I truly believed in my heart that we had
something significant, something worth
fighting the rest of our lives for.

   - like we always said we would

I feel like I've lost everything
my life was building up to, as if
this story of mine truly has no
happy ending.

   - *such a sad summer*

What hurts the most about
feeling this way about you is,
I never thought I'd ever have
to feel this way about you.

- I never saw it coming

We always had
moments in the clouds
followed by moments of
pure, utter lowness. And
love should not have *so many*
steep hills and deep valleys.

   - inconsistently happy

It's just so hard to believe that with all this love,
I still wasn't able to keep you from being unhappy.
And people tell me it wasn't my fault, that people
with sharp edges have to go dull on their own, but
I often find myself still carrying around the weight
of feeling responsible for all of this.

- I tried to save you

What messes me up the most is
how you left when we still had
so many reasons to stay.

I knew you weren't in love
when I saw it in your eyes that you
were completely okay with me
falling asleep unhappy.

If I woke up one day,
and I was ten years old again,
I'd lose so many things, but it'd
be worth it because I could
be with you again.

*- someday, we'd meet, and
we could try all over again*

My life hit a rough patch,
and you left because of that,
as if me dealing with my pain
was too much of a burden
for you to bear, as if the
"through anything" we
always told each other
never meant a thing.

  - *so much for soulmates*

A year of my life later,
and I have nothing to show
for it but these scars – these
worries that no matter how
long you've known someone,
at any moment they
can still leave.

- the impressions leaving leaves

Some days, it feels as if my life has a limit on
how much happiness I can feel. And when that
limit is reached, it has to be drained out until I
can be happy again. It seems to come and go in
these cycles, these seasons of bliss followed shorty
by these seasons of numbness, sadness, or pain.
And it makes me wonder if anything can
truly last forever.

   - the sadness that makes us question everything

You'd never let anything
get in the way of your happiness,
not even my sadness. And I sometimes
found myself wondering if that is
truly how love is supposed to be.

   - *when one person matters more*

I can't put into words
just how it feels when the
person you love tells you
you'll find someone
who loves you.

   - *some kind of sinking*

You're not here anymore,
and now clouds hang over
all of the places that used
to make me feel warm.

- it hurts to go where we've been

What I miss the most
isn't you, necessarily; what
I miss more than anything is
how happy you made me feel
at first with myself and my life
and where it was headed. I had
dreams, and you were in them.
I felt at peace, and it was
all because of you.

- *love in its infancy*

We were perfect at first,
way back then before we
started being ourselves.

I've never actually known
what true love is: all I know
is that I've always been told
I need more of it.

And so I've searched for
all of my life, for something I
don't even know the shape of,
for something that may not
even be out there for me
to bring back home.

   - the loneliest journey

In late nights, I
torture myself with
these questions I
know will never
have answers.

- like why you left

I spent so much time
suffering over how unhappy
I was with you, I failed to see
how unhappy that must have
made you. It was wrong. It was
selfish. It's something I wish
I never made you feel.

   - *where I went wrong*

Going into Autumn Alone

I'm tired of getting back up just
to get knocked back down again.
And they say the ability to get back
up is necessary in this life, but what
they never told me is that this is how
I'd be spending most of my youth,
bouncing in and out of happiness.

- no youth to look back on

I was an unhappy person,
and some days, I can feel
myself going back to being that
old person again. And nothing
feels worse than that, knowing
you're free-falling backwards
with no energy left to do
anything about it.

You said I'd need to change
if you were to stay in my life,
as if who I'd always been with you
wasn't the person you fell in love with.
And in the end, I was left all alone with
the question, "who the hell have I just
wasted all of this time on?"

- when summer closed its eyes

And suddenly,
my mornings became
coffee and wishing all
of this never happened.

I can't help but feel
that we missed out on
sixty-plus years of
happiness together,
all because of
terrible timing.

  - *this curse of ours*

We saw adulthood in the distance;
it looked like a light. For years, we
walked toward it, just to arrive there
one day to find that it was nice, but it
was less than what we hoped for.

It's all we have now, though: in exchange
for the freedom of being older, we traded
in the happiness of our younger days. And
now, we look back fondly and longingly
on that bliss and think to ourselves,
"I really had it good, didn't I?"

    - the grass is always greener

One day,
I woke up to the
undeniable realization
that things between us
would never be the same.

- and still, I stayed

What's so confusing is that you fell off
the face of the Earth, but I never did anything
to make you want to never see my face again.
And so I'm left here with half the story, trying
to piece together something, anything, that
makes some kind of sense to me.

Most nights, I come up with nothing –
left to assume that maybe I just wasn't
good enough to make you want to stay.

- filling in the blanks for you

My dreams have fallen
from the clouds and landed
on top of my back, crushing
my tired soul completely.

And now, I'm just stumbling
my way through this life of mine,
hoping that I can someday find
the strength and courage to pick
myself up and start over again.

But doing this is hard when you
have lost all faith in good things
and their ability to stay in your
life forever.

After watching what you thought
would never leave you slam the door
behind it as if you never meant a thing,
I don't think you're ever quite the same
person you were ever again.

So now, I'm just here, hoping that
never being the same person again will
somehow be the best thing to ever
had happened to me someday.

I await this this day.
I long for this closure.

- standing back up

I weave dreams out of
the idea of you coming back,
interlace yesterday and tomorrow
with your old and empty
promises of forever.

False hope has always been
the only hope I've ever known
when it comes to you and I.

- thinking of us

I stopped looking in
the mirror as much after you:
it's not because you made me
feel unbeautiful; it's the fact
that every time I see myself,
I'm reminded of the fact
that I only used to be a
person you once saw as
worthy of loving.

I've seen dreams so big
slip through the smallest
cracks between my fingers.

I've seen love die quietly
on a Tuesday night at 8pm,
and the world didn't even
stop to say it's sorry.

You end some things the
same way you began them:
all by yourself.

No one comes to put you
out of your misery; no, things
and dreams die out quietly,
and it's up to you to pull
yourself out of the cold
and lonely wreckage
before it's too late.

- shipwrecked

By the end of us, I had been
coated in the fear of losing you,
and I shouldn't have had to live
my life worrying about whether
or not your heart would still
be there when I woke up
in the morning.

Looking back,
those acts of affection
had no meaning, but in
my head, packed tightly
with loneliness, I filled in
the gaps and convinced
myself that what we
had was love when
it truly wasn't.

- *the first time I felt disposable*

I moved mountains,
and you complained
about the view. And it
was in that moment when
I realized, something
had to change.

You said things changed,
that you didn't feel the same
way anymore. And that didn't
really take my breath away,
because you can't stay in
love forever if you were
never truly in it in
the first place.

*- I already knew you didn't love me;
  I just hoped someday you would.*

Our love was like falling
into deep water, treading without
the knowhow to swim. And only if
we had given up, surrendered the fear
of drowning and stopped fighting it,
would we have realized that we can float –
just be in love without even trying.

  -trying to make it work made it worse

I bet my heart on
the off chance that
you would someday
look at me the way
I'd always wanted.

- *the day that never came*

And so here I lay, trying to understand why there's
a difference between what I see and what people tell me,
why I feel so unhappy with myself even though people
seem so convinced I am worthy of love. It's like I hold
two ropes in my hands, and everything would be okay
if I could just tie a knot that connects them together. But,
I just don't know how to do that; I just don't understand
how to move my hands in a way that leads to me
feeling good about myself again.

- if only I had an angel

Sometimes,
I feel bad for the old me -
as if, if they knew who I
turned out to be, they
wouldn't be excited
to turn life's pages.

I'll be here waiting,
until the next good news
comes along to make me
feel better for a little while.

- too tired to move

What's so sad is that
I've never asked for much:
all I've ever really wanted is
someone I can truly rely on.

I could run for years,
but I'd still end up right
back where I started off.

And no matter how happy
this world makes me, I always
return to that same sad place
that's been inside of me
since I was a child.

  - believe me, I've tried to run

It's dark out -
starless skies above me.

I shut my phone off
(nobody is getting to me).

I shut my eyes and think of nothing
(not even myself).

For now, this is what peace is to me,
but it won't always have to be this way.

I know this. I know this for a fact:
I won't always be running away.

  - faith with no proof to back it up

I need hope again.

There is no rain to drown out
the sound of my thoughts at night.

I close my eyes and find no peace,
just to open them again and see no
end to this drought in sight.

It used to rain here often.
Where has the rainwater gone?

Clouds once formed and lifted into
the skyline of my bedroom ceiling.

They'd rain a wonderful water,
and the drops would sing me to sleep,
but the rainwater left when you did.

And now, it's just quiet.

If you wont see my importance,
I wont stick around and try to
convince you that it exists.

My greatest hope tonight
is that someday I'll look
back on these tears and see
that they served a purpose.

- this is all I ask

I understand that I
have to feel pain; what
I don't understand is why
I have to feel it so much.

- *far too many heartbreaks*

I could not
bear the loudness
of being let down,
so I made the world
quieter by cutting
everyone I knew
out of it.

- *the quietest quiet*

Everything
would've been okay,
if only you had the heart
to tell your mind, *"no, this
is still what I want; this is still
all I've always asked for."*

- you thought your way out of love

My heart is broken,
and you're oblivious to it,
and sometimes I still wish
that were different.

- you moved on like I don't exist

I'm getting better
about missing you,
but sometimes, your
sweater still keeps
me warm at night.

- it smells like you, too

Sometimes, I feel like
it's not all your fault or
even most of it: maybe I
stopped doing the things
that made you fall
in love with me.

Feelings change:
we know this, but we
cast it aside and make
exceptions for the people
we so tragically want
to love us forever.

What killed me about
seeing you be so cold
to me in the end was
remembering how you
were so kind to me
in the beginning.

Some days, I see myself as being
so close to the opposite of beautiful,
I find it hard to believe that anybody
could ever look at me and see
something worth fighting for.

Sometimes,
I cut people off,
because the guilt of
missing you while getting
to know someone new
is too much to take.

I'm starting
to realize lately:
I don't miss you;
I miss who I
thought
you were.

You had this incredible ability to
convince me that everything wrong
between us was all my fault. And in my
desperate need to keep you around, I
let this go on until I hated who I was.

- suffering in silence

My heart took the wheel
and fell asleep behind it.
And, suddenly, all I knew
was that I was in love,
and I was unhappy.

   - *with closed eyes*

Slowly but surely, it happened. And it took
so long to happen, I didn't even see it coming.
I just woke up one day, and suddenly I realized
there were these walls around my life. And these
walls were so high, I couldn't see over them; all I
could do was sit in this isolation and remember
what my life used to be like.

- quietly, you rearranged my life

You were beautiful back then.
I sometimes find myself wondering
if you're still beautiful today. Then
again, how could you not be?

- snow on white wings

Sometimes,
someone changes
your life; other times,
someone destroys it.

    - sad we met

I'm just hurting myself
more as the days go on,
continuing to put off getting
over you. But being hurt over
this makes me feel closer to the
moment we ended, and I'd do
anything just to be closer
to you again.

   - *any kind of closer*

If you understood me, tried a little bit harder
to get into my head, you never would have left.
It's just easier to believe what you want to believe.
It's just a simpler thing to blame everybody but
yourself and run away. You took the easy way out
while I stood there alone ready to fight for us, but
you can't save something that takes two people
to save when you're all by yourself.

But so it goes, we are forever un-savable now,
and all I can do today is try to get on with my life –
try to find closure and keep my head up
in any way I can.

Morning Light

What if it's tomorrow?
What if that's when my life
finally turns around?

What if all I need to do is
hang on just one day longer?

I take a deep breath, ask myself
these questions, and fall asleep
with hope curled up next to me.

It's enough for now,
and enough is all I've
ever needed.

- tighten your grip: stay

The pain will settle in,
burrow into your chest
and make itself a home there.
And you won't know what to
do with it for a while, but you'll
hold on anyways, because there's
always hope that, someday,
maybe you will.

There's no salt for wounds of the soul.
There's no quick fix or other way around it.
You have to go through it, feel it, every little
bit of it. You have to suffer, cry your eyes out,
not want to get out of bed, miss them as if they
were a part of you that you will never get back.
Because that's what it is, isn't it? Is that not what
we do? Give pieces of ourselves away to people
and hope they never choose to run away?

- the beautiful things we do

They'll tell you to move on.
They'll tell you to do things you love.
They'll tell you to make new dreams.
They'll tell you to make new friends.
They'll tell you to see old friends, too.

But they wont tell you the single
most important part: to face the pain,
to look straight at it and say,

*"I am stronger than you. I will
get over you and become a happier person
again when I am done carving you
out of my heart and soul."*

- pulling at the roots

I'm still bothered by how
you got the better of me,
but I just don't think that's
something I should be feeling
anymore: today, letting you go
seems like the best thing for me.

- today, I'll carry on

Even if I never
get over us completely,
I have to at least somehow
learn to be thankful for
all I've learned from
our time together.

I'm sure
there's good in this
goodbye somewhere;
I'm sure I just haven't
found it quite yet.

 - *a reason for this*

For now,
I'll think about it
most of the time and
forget about it long enough
to be happy every now and then.
It won't always be this way, but,
for now, it is this way. And I have
to learn how to be okay with that.

It's at times like this where
I stop and think, "if I don't deal
with the pain now, someday, it'll
come back to haunt me." And so
I bury myself in it - rage war against
running away and choose to stay,
choosing to feel it all.

- blood in the bathwater

My mother embraced me
when she got home from work.
I cried in her arms as she told me,
"*it will be okay.*" I didn't believe her then,
but in that moment, something told me
that maybe someday I would.

- in loving arms

I'd give anything
to feel that happiness
you made me feel again,
even if it means finding it
all on my own, somewhere
inside of myself.

   - *it was incredible*

It doesn't hit me like it used to hit me. It happens
every now and then. In the middle of living my life,
I'll remember what happened. I'll remember that my world
has a void in it now. Sometimes, my heart sinks - most times,
it doesn't. And a part of me feels guilty for learning to let go
of something I once felt I could never afford to lose.

But mostly, I'm just glad that I can be happy without what
used to be the root of my happiness. My only hope now is that
I never start to remember only the good things, because that
will make me miss us all over again, and I've come too far
to forget all of the reasons I had to get on with my life.

- the heart and its will to keep beating

Yeah, I miss you,
but I don't want the
pain only being with
you brings again.

Let's be honest,
we were great when
we got along, but those
great moments were
too few and far
between.

One day, I decided I just can't live my life
hoping that my past comes back and makes me
feel the way it used to make me feel. And even
if it did come back, it's been places other than
somewhere with me, and I don't think my
heart could ever handle such a heavy
weight on top of it.

- leaving what needs to be left

If my past
were different,
I would be different.
And today, I don't
think that's such
a beautiful idea.

- *loving who I am*

I'm learning to control
my reactions to the world
around me, how to not let
other people's decisions
change the way I feel.

   - *turning inward*

They'll throw words at you. They'll make you feel like you're worth next to nothing. They'll get angry when they pull at the strings they've tied around you and see that you don't budge. They'll threaten you with leaving. You'll start allowing them to conduct your every move because you don't want to fight again - because them saying things like "I want someone who does this" and "if you love me, you'll do this" is starting to get to your head.

You'll begin to change, and it won't feel right. This uneasiness will boil inside of you. You'll get angry at letting someone walk over you and change your life in such a messed up way. And, one day, you'll snap. You'll lose your mind and fight back.

They'll do one of two things: fight with you until the bloody end or walk right out of your life, making it all feel like it's your fault. And let me tell you something, it is your fault...that they're gone, and it's something you should be terribly proud of.

You stood up for yourself. You fought back, and no matter how they try to make you feel about it all, I need you to remember that you made the right decision.

In my head, there is a room. A room with no windows, just bricks on every wall, a wooden chair, and a fireplace. Above this fireplace hangs six symbols against the bricks, one for every self-defeating way of thinking I've had the strength to overcome: anger over the past, comparing myself to others, thinking that I am not beautiful, feeling less than useful when remembering who I used to be, and worrying that I don't have much left to offer this world. But I am not done yet: there is much space left within this room and many worriments left to place against these bricks.

- the tomb of unhappier times

I'm still not sure what went wrong with us:
I guess, you just got tired of trying to mold me
into somebody else while framing it as wanting
the best for me. I guess, you got what I could give
and went on with your life. And I'm coming to
terms with that; it's just a little hard some days
to get the memories of you telling me I am
not enough out of my head.

- when it rains, I remember

It's so hard
to feel this lonely,
but it's not as bad
as the hatred I felt
for myself when we
were together.

- I'd rather feel this

You made me feel
new things when I was
convinced I'd felt it all.
Why should I ever look
back in anger at that?

- like a kid again

Somewhere along the way,
I decided that losing you wouldn't
be the end of me, and that was the
single most important decision
I'd ever made in my life.

You'd ask why I seem
so down, so uninspired,
and I never had it in me to
tell you that this relationship
was literally sucking the
life right out of me.

I don't want you back,
and I don't need you in my
daily life: I just wish we were
at least on speaking terms – the
kind where you meet up every
once in a while and get drunk
together on our favorite,
old memories.

Pain has wings.
It was not made to stay
in one place forever.

It will leave you someday,
and you'll be a better person
because of its arrival.

- pain, the angel

Surround yourself with people
who would wait outside the gates
of heaven for as long as it'd take
for you to arrive.

   - it's not heaven without you

If you love something,
embrace it, and never apologize
for those things your arms
are wrapped around.

- life's too short

I loved the idea of
being happy so much,
one day, I became it.

- become what you love

Build a space in your heart
that only you can enter, and you
can love freely knowing you'll
always have a little left over
for yourself.

I emotionally detached
before you left, because
I'd gotten sick of and had
grown numb to your constant,
violent threats of leaving.

   - *why I seem okay*

I can't blame it all on you;
in the end, I think we both
let each other down in
ways of our own.

- *expecting wind from water*

Everyday, I practice grace,
water it as if it were a flower -
as if, if I didn't do this, I'd
wither away the garden in
my heart I've spent my
entire life growing.

- fields of flowers

At least I can say
I had the bravery to stay
and try to fight for us when
all you wanted to do was
give up on all we built.

The ones who stay,
those are the ones who
should matter the most.

- not the ones who leave

We were always almost perfect –
right there on the edge of it, so close
we could almost touch it. And I don't
think either of us truly wanted the torture
of spending even just one more day being
a stone's throw away from happiness.

- a heartbreaking almost

Someday, I'll be happy,
and I'll be okay. I just need
some time to work on the
picture I have of myself
inside of my head.

A Reason to Keep Breathing

I'm choosing to look at us ending
as the start of something. And though
I'm only one step out of our grave,
the view is already beautiful.

I think it's finally time to drop my guard and take a look at myself, work on my soul until it looks how it was always meant to look. I know there's a better person somewhere inside of me. I know there's more growing to be had. And for the first time in my life, I'm truly ready to become that person.

One day, I realized that
I was just repeating the same
relationship with different
people, and that was when
I decided it was time to
try something different.

- I don't want to feel this again

It doesn't hit me like it used to hit me. It happens every now and then. In the middle of living my life, I'll remember what happened. I'll remember that my world has a void in it now. Sometimes, my heart sinks - most times, it doesn't.

And a part of me feels guilty for learning to let go of something I once felt I could never afford to lose. But mostly, I'm just glad that I can be happy without what used to be the root of my happiness.

My only hope now is that I never start to remember only the good things, because that will make me miss us all over again, and I've come too far to forget all of the reasons I had to get on with my life.

"What comes next?"
once was a question that
used to haunt me, but now,
it's a question that fills
my heart with hope.

   - high hopes

When you feel the most
lost you've ever felt, smile
knowing that right before
you find some direction is
usually right after you've
completely lost your way.

Do yourself a favor:
listen to the people
who have survived
your pain; soak up
everything they've
got to say about it.

   - let it help you

Someday, your heart will take it easy on you,
be more understanding and forgiving. And when
that happens, you'll truly begin to forgive yourself
for the things you have caused to leave. Because,
you can try to convince yourself a thousand times
that you forgive yourself, but it won't work until
your heart truly believes it.

In the end, really,
what is love other than
a gateway into a new,
more-beautiful way
of looking at
the world.

  - *love's viewpoint*

If your heart and soul hurt,
that just means you care. And if
you still care in a world like this,
consider yourself lucky that you
have not been abandoned by
what makes you human.

If someone were
to ask me what falling
in love feels like, I'd say,
"as if you were born with wings,
and after all of this time, you just
now discovered that you were born
with the ability to take flight."

I want to be mad that we lost
all of this love, but a part of me
knows that I was lucky to have felt
something so real in the first place.

- for a while, we had what people wish for

I ran from unhappiness for years, the misery of
placing my heart in someone else's hands and hoping
they never choose to squeeze. But I put my faith in you,
built up the nerve by receiving warm words and acts of
love that all hinted at the existence of something honest
and everlasting. Into love, I leapt. And in the free-fall,
slowly but surely the unhappiness caught right back up
to me, almost as if it belonged with me. And I'm sorry for
the way my pain came between us. Sometimes, I wish
I knew how to deal with it all back then.

Pay close attention,
because more than anything,
what will tell you the most about
someone is the way they make
you feel when you're wrong
about something.

Someday,
you'll find someone
who will never break
your heart and will
always stay.

We'll say we don't
want love right now,
but I think, secretly, a
part of us always keeps
a little bit of space in our
heart for someone who
can turn our world
upside down.

I don't remember much.
It was March. It was cold.
You were beautiful.

   - all I know for certain

I'm not usually one to
reminisce on the past and smile,
but we have these memories now,
and sometimes, I catch myself
smiling as I lay in bed at night
and stare off into empty space.

  - as if stars were in my bedroom

Days were darker then,
so I believed even harder
because of it: no lack of light
was ever going to make me
have a lack of hope.

   - *how hope reacts to darkness*

I grew tired of getting hurt,
so I hid myself away and made
people climb mountains to get
to my trust. And while I thought
I was weeding out all the people
undeserving of my heart, all I
was truly doing was causing
my own loneliness.

You are kind. You are thoughtful –
those of you who take the blame to
keep it away from the ones you love.
But it's time to be kind and
thoughtful to yourself.

You've seen other people be
happy without you, move on
with their lives and still find
happiness. Good. Now you
know that it's possible; now
you know that you
can do it, too.

I woke up feeling like
I could be anything,
so, today, I chose
to be happier.

- leaving things behind

A positive mindset
is the richest of all soils
to plant your dreams in.

I miss the way
knowing I had you
always had the power
to breathe life into me
when I was so close
to giving up.

- *for what it's worth*

What I've learned from us is,
if you be yourself from the first hello,
you'll never have to wonder if you're
loved for who you truly are.

Life got better the day
I understood that in any
given moment, I could be
just one breath away from
the happiest moment
of my life.

  - one breath away

I'm not the type to say
I've been better, even if I've
been better. I'd much rather
take a chisel to my soul and
sculpt something that more
closely resembles who
I want to be.

- let's not talk about it

I've cut so many people out of my life;
this fact saddens me to my very core. And
though it's taken me years to realize this,
I've come to understand that just because
I'm lost in this world, it doesn't mean
I have to be alone in it.

Be honest with yourself:
every time you tell yourself
you're happy when you aren't,
you teach yourself how to be
better at living a lie.

If there is beauty in the way
stars destroy themselves, I'm
entirely convinced there is
some beauty to be had in the
way we had to fall apart.

You don't wake up one day and
suddenly your soul is made of stone.

The path to unhappiness is a gentle slope,
a gradual adding of weight onto your soul.

It's a series of daily choices to accept how you
feel, doing nothing to change the mood you're in.

It's choosing to be still, dead water when
you were born with every right to be a river.

It's making statements about who you are instead
of asking questions about who you could be.

But you were not born to be unhappy,
so stop acting like you are out of options.

Let this moment be the one you talk about
when someone someday asks you about
how you got to where you are.

- wind for the soul's sails

It's only a matter of time
until time no longer matters.
It's not "if," but "when"
we all meet our end.

Make use of your time
before it's too late.

Do today what you must,
so you can be okay with going
to sleep knowing you might
not wake up tomorrow.

Build that dream.
Get that closure.
Find that forgiveness
while you're still
around to forgive.

- a lifetime is just a moment

We were an intersection
into each other's life, a short
meeting before a long and
unending separation.

 - *temporary but necessary*

As I grow older,
I find myself longing for
subsurface connections,
intertwining souls with
people who plan on
sticking around.

- soul friends only

Happiness is when
dreaming about other lives
wherein things worked out
differently is no longer
something you do.

- *happier here*

Looking back,
I don't think it was love:
I was just obsessed with
solving problems, and
you had a lot of them.

  - soul custodian

I chose to be here.
I chose to open my heart
and take on the risk of ending up
broken. I saw a great, beautiful love
and deemed it worthy enough of
maybe losing everything. And I
can't hate myself now for, at one
point in time, choosing to be brave.

- I was pushed from no cliffs; I jumped

Remember this: even
if the world around you
is hopeless, that doesn't
mean you have to feel
hopeless, too.

Listen. I know your heart hurts. I know it feels like you can't go on. And maybe even a part of you knows that life will go on, but you might not want it to right now. I'm telling you, someday, you'll be so damn glad that you held on, that you chose to be here. So hold on for dear life, because, someday, you'll be stronger because this happened, and you'll be thankful to your old self for making it through these days.

Never lose hope
that tomorrow just
might be the one
that changes
everything.

It begins with minutes: one here; one there. You relish
in them, tranquility has saved you from torment...for a
moment. It's small, but it's a start. And you take notice of
the fact that even after pain, utterly heart wrenching misery,
you can still feel peace - happiness even. You've seen some
kind of brightness, the glorious returning of morning light
inside your soul. For now, it's still dark in there, but those
minutes begin to add up - their lives extending upward and
outward into hours, days, weeks. And before you even know
it, more days are spent smiling than spent curled up in bed
with the lights out. Your soul will return to the happiness it
used to know, and someday, I'm sure of this, your days will
begin to be even brighter than they ever were before.

- a reason to keep breathing